P9-DUX-705

BLAST OFF INTO THE UNKNOWN WITH . . .

SCIENTISTS
in ACTION!

Astronauts!

MC

SCIENTISTS in ACTION!

Archaeologists!

Astronauts!

Big-Animal Vets!

Biomedical Engineers!

Civil Engineers!

Climatologists!

Crime Scene Techs!

Cyber Spy Hunters!

Marine Biologists!

Robot Builders!

Astronauts!

By K.C. Kelley

Mason Crest
450 Parkway Drive, Suite D
Broomall, PA 19008
www.masoncrest.com

Printed and bound in the United States of America.

Series ISBN: 978-1-4222-3416-7
Hardback ISBN: 978-1-4222-3418-1
EBook ISBN: 978-1-4222-8479-7

First printing
1 3 5 7 9 8 6 4 2

Produced by Shoreline Publishing Group LLC
Santa Barbara, California
Editorial Director: James Buckley Jr.
Designer: Tom Carling, Carling Design Inc.
Production: Sandy Gordon
www.shorelinepublishing.com
Cover image: NASA

Library of Congress Cataloging-in-Publication Data
Kelley, K. C., author.
        Astronauts! / by K.C. Kelley.
                pages cm. -- (Scientists in action!) Audience: Grades 9-12.
Includes bibliographical references and index.
ISBN 978-1-4222-3418-1 (hardback : alk. paper) -- ISBN 978-1-4222-3416-7 (series : alk. paper) -- ISBN
978-1-4222-8479-7 (ebook) 1. Astronauts--Juvenile literature. 2. Astronautics--Juvenile literature. 3. Outer
space--Exploration--Juvenile literature. I. Title.
TL793.K43 2015
629.45--dc23
                                2015004672

Contents

Key Icons to Look For

 Words to Understand: These words with their easy-to-understand definitions will increase the reader's understanding of the text, while building vocabulary skills.

 Sidebars: This boxed material within the main text allows readers to build knowledge, gain insights, explore possibilities, and broaden their perspectives by weaving together additional information to provide realistic and holistic perspectives.

 Research Projects: Readers are pointed toward areas of further inquiry connected to each chapter. Suggestions are provided for projects that encourage deeper research and analysis.

 Text-Dependent Questions: These questions send the reader back to the text for more careful attention to the evidence presented here.

 Series Glossary of Key Terms: This back-of-the-book glossary contains terminology used throughout this series. Words found here increase the reader's ability to read and comprehend higher-level books and articles in this field.

Action!

D r. Thomas Marshburn (pictured at left) was a college professor, but at this moment in the spring of 2013, he was a looong way from the classroom. Years earlier, he had spent many years studying hard to become a medical doctor. He also had a degree in physics. He had become a teacher to pass on what he had learned along the way. So why was he floating 200 miles (321 km) above the Earth, wearing a space suit and facing a pressure-packed situation? Because Marshburn was a scientist and an astronaut. As the Earth spun below him, Marshburn had to call on all of his skills to help save his fellow astronauts.

WORDS TO UNDERSTAND

airlock   a room on a space station from which astronauts can move from inside to outside the station and back

ammonia   a gas used in refrigeration; can be deadly if inhaled

Marshburn had grown up in North Carolina and Georgia. After attending four different schools to study science and medicine, he had worked as an emergency-room doctor. On that job, he had to deal with sudden problems, and had to make fast decisions. He did not have time to get rattled when a car-crash victim came in for help. He had to get the work done, no matter what.

He then took a job using his medical expertise to help the space program, making sure future astronauts were healthy and ready for space. After a while, he decided to make the big leap himself and become an astronaut, too!

After taking tests and doing interviews, he became an astronaut in 2004. In 2009, he flew aboard the space shuttle *Endeavour*; his astronaut dream had come true! His mission was to deliver parts and experiments to the International Space Station (ISS). During that time, he took his first space walks, working outside the station for more than 18 hours. That experience would come in handy later on.

In 2013, he was chosen for another mission—to live on the ISS for six months! While living with astronauts from Canada and Russia, Marshburn helped them stay healthy while he also did important scientific research. He learned to eat his meals while floating in zero gravity. He had to sleep in a bag stuck to a wall. He went six months without a real shower, using only handy wipes to clean up. Still, he loved every minute of it.

On May 11, 2013, just a few days before he was to come home, there was a problem. **Ammonia**, a dangerous gas, was leaking into the space station. There was only one way to fix it: time for a space walk.

Usually space walks are planned for months, and every possible situation is covered. NASA had not tried such a sudden space walk before. Anything could go wrong due to the lack of planning. Now, however, there was no time to wait. The doctor from Georgia had to pull on his space suit and head out into the icy blackness to save the day.

Marshburn and fellow astronaut Christopher Cassidy moved into the **airlock** on board the ISS. They had spent the previous few hours going over their tasks. Teams on the ground had shown them what to do, and they looked at diagrams of what they would find outside. Outside the window, they could see small chips of frozen ammonia leaking into space. If that leak turned around and leaked inside the station, it could be very dangerous for the men living aboard. The ammonia also helped keep power grids cool. Without that power, some of the

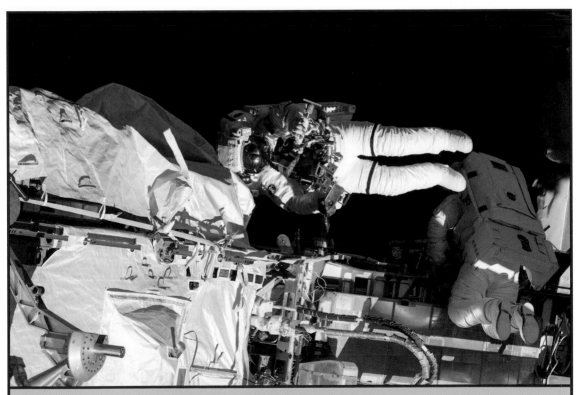

After putting on his space suit, Marshburn went through the airlock and into the freezing, airless environment outside the International Space Station.

Using hand tools strapped to his suit (so they did not float away), Marshburn made careful repairs to a broken pump that would keep the astronauts inside the station safe from harm.

important scientific experiments on board might be damaged. There was no more time to wait.

The two astronauts gathered their tools and waited for the airlock to open. After attaching safety lines to the station itself, they stepped into space.

The two men clung to the outside of the station as it whizzed through space. They could look down and see clouds covering the land. As they continued their orbit, oceans came into view. Whole mountain ranges were visible. It was an amazing sight, but they had to get to work.

Other astronauts watched from inside the station, while on the ground far below, NASA experts looked on helplessly.

It was up to the floating doctor to save the day.

Wearing bulky gloves but using delicate tools, the two men carefully installed a new pump that would stop the leak. Marshburn was used to working in pressure situations. This was like life back in the ER . . . in zero gravity.

Though his wrench was tied to his glove, Marshburn still held on tightly. Then he carefully tightened the last bolt. Marshburn and Cassidy watched carefully for many minutes to see if any more ammonia leaked out. The situation was tense, but Marshburn remained cool and calm.

Finally, after testing the pump, the word came through: All clear! No more leak!

When Thomas Marshburn was working as a doctor, he probably never thought that one day he would become a scientist in space! Now he was one of dozens of men and women who had taken their love of science to new heights . . . really, really high new heights!

The Scientists and Their Science

*I*magine if you were a scientist . . . and your laboratory was 250 miles (400 km) above the Earth. That's the case for many of the men and women who have lived and worked on American space shuttles and at the ISS. Science is a major reason for space exploration, so scientists need to go where the action is!

On space shuttle missions and on the ISS, scientists of all kinds work in zero gravity. They perform experiments in many branches of science, learning how humans can live in space. Some of the things they have learned while working as astronauts have helped make life on Earth better. Scientists are a huge part of the world's space exploration programs.

WORDS TO UNDERSTAND

cosmonauts   space travelers from the Soviet Union or Russia

meteorology   the study of weather

physicists   scientists who study physics, which examines how matter and energy move and relate

That was not always true. When the space programs in the United States and Russia began in the early 1960s, all the first space travelers were from the military. Astronauts (from the United States) and **cosmonauts** (from the Soviet Union) needed to be pilots first and explorers second. Flying the huge rockets and then steering the small capsules called for skills that scientists just didn't have. Early space missions were super-dangerous, and experienced pilots were ready for any flying emergency.

The first Mercury 7 astronauts, for example, were all pilots. John Glenn, the first man to orbit Earth, was a decorated fighter pilot from the U.S. Marines. Neil Armstrong and Buzz Aldrin, the first men on the moon, were U.S. Air Force pilots who had flown in combat. Russia's Yuri Gagarin, the first man in space in 1961, had flown in the Soviet Air Forces.

In 1965, however, NASA decided to bring scientists to the science. They hired six new astronauts who were scientists first and pilots second. Four of those men later worked in space. It was the beginning of a new chapter for space exploration. While pilots were still needed, and many astronauts still came from the different branches of the U.S. military, more and more people headed to space for science.

The American astronauts, all military pilots, who kicked off the space program for NASA came to be known as the Mercury 7, after the name of the spacecraft they would fly.

Over the next decades, more and more scientists were sent into space. Each space shuttle mission included people called mission specialists. Most of them were not pilots, but were sent into orbit to conduct experiments. They had started their scientific careers on Earth . . . but they would continue them in space!

Science in Space

Just about any branch of science can be studied in space. The way that astronauts reach space started with science, of course. Rockets were created by engineers using ideas from **physicists**. Scientists who study the motion of planets and the moon had to show how those rockets should be launched to end up back on Earth. When NASA aimed at a moon landing, astronomers had to find where the moon would be—exactly—so that the launch times would be made at just the right moments.

Even meteorologists, people who study weather, were part of the space flight team. They had to make sure that the skies would be clear for safe launches. Several times, their predictions of storms kept astronauts from blasting off into lightning.

Science has long been a vital part of the entire space program. With the addition of scientists into the astronaut corps, that work blasted off. People who had studied physics, engineering, biology, and other sciences found that their skills were needed off-planet.

A big reason for this need was the idea that humans would be living in space a lot in the future. How would that affect them and their bodies?

Scientists became living labs as they worked on this problem. Medical doctors were part of some missions, so they could study how the other astronauts reacted to life in space. Biologists who study living things watched as plants and insects grew in space. Knowing how to grow crops for food during future space missions might be very valuable. Future astronauts might be able to grow their own food while they travel to distant lands.

The study of weather is called **meteorology**. Experts in that science can spin above the Earth and study weather patterns, winds, storms, and hurricanes.

Chemistry experts did experiments to watch how compounds and elements reacted to space conditions. Would they react as they do on on Earth? Or would the lack of gravity affect how they mixed or reacted?

The emerging eye of a hurricane takes on its well-known spiral shape in this image taken from the ISS. Studying weather from space gives scientists a new way to look at how weather moves on Earth.

Even oceanographers can learn in space. By looking down from the space station, they can see huge areas of the ocean. Special cameras can record the growth of algae in the water, or can see how currents move.

Engineers, of course, find lots to do in space. They help operate and maintain the ISS, while also trying out new gear to see how it works in space. The lessons they take back to Earth will help make future missions better and safer.

Being an astronaut certainly includes the excitement of launch and the wonder of seeing Earth from space. It also means using scientific knowledge to help everyone.

Becoming an Astronaut

ow does a scientist become an astronaut? The first step: Send in an application! Just about any college graduate can apply to be an astronaut, but it is a very selective process. In many countries around the world, thousands of people try out for just a few spots. You have to be an expert in your field, but you also have to be willing to train and work hard. You will probably sacrifice time with your family or have to move to where the space programs need you to train. Plus, of course, there is danger involved. In the past 50 years, 30 astronauts have lost their lives due to accidents.

Astronaut training starts on Earth, of course. Here, an astronaut practices moving around in a harness that mimics working in the zero gravity of space.

If you think you have, as they say, "the right stuff," though, go for it! U.S. citizens apply through NASA, while military service members start with their branch of the military. People who live in countries that are part of the European Space Agency (including France, the Netherlands, Italy, Spain, and Germany, among others), as well as citizens of Canada, Japan, Russia, and Brazil apply in their own nations.

If your application is accepted, you'll undergo many

Chris Hadfield of Canada flew on five missions and was the first Canadian to walk in space.

tests. Your background will be carefully checked to make sure you have what the first astronauts called the "right stuff." The people hiring astronauts will interview you to make sure you will be someone willing to live in tight quarters with people. If you're on the ISS for three months, there's no way to go for a walk to get away from a grumpy co-worker! Also, today's space programs connect astronauts from many countries. Your nation will make sure you can study languages and learn to work with people from other cultures. In fact, speaking another language (such as Russian or Japanese) will make you a better candidate.

To be an astronaut, a scientist has to be smart . . . but also in great shape. Astronaut candidates will take many physical tests. They have to be healthy and able to withstand the hard work of getting ready for

Why I Became an Astronaut

"I can't remember a time when I didn't want to be an astronaut," said Janet Kavandi. "I saw all the stars at night, and I remember talking with my dad about what it would look like from 'up there.'" She earned advanced degrees in chemistry, but always wanted to see what life was like in space. "I worked hard in math and science, but always had my eye on making that dream come true."

Kavandi was accepted as an astronaut in 1994 and her dream came true on her first mission in 1998. She later went back to space twice more, having spent 33 days in space as a high-flying chemist.

Janet Kavandi trained as a chemist, but later saw her dreams of space flight come true.

launch, as well as the rough ride into space. Then they need to keep that good health for months in space. If an astronaut got seriously ill way up there, help is far away.

One other thing to keep in mind: If you're too tall or too short (as an adult!), you might not qualify. Because of the tight spaces astronauts might have to go, there is a height limit of 6 feet 3 inches (1.9 m). You also need to be at least 5 feet 2 inches (1.57 m) to make sure you'll fit into the suits, gear, and other protective devices.

Also, be a good swimmer. You'll be "swimming" in space in zero gravity. People who are not good swimmers will not make good or safe astronauts.

With so many people wanting to be astronauts, not everyone is chosen. Engineer Michael Massimino applied four times before he was chosen in 1996. He later flew on missions in 2002 and 2009. Persistence pays off, even when becoming an astronaut.

Once you have passed all the tests and they have a spot for you, you're in. However, you're not really an astronaut until you make that first journey into space. You'll experience the wonder of spaceflight . . . and then it will be time to get to work. There's science to be done!

Text-Dependent Questions

1. What does an American need to apply to be an astronaut?
2. Who was the first man to orbit the Earth?
3. Name one country that is part of the European Space Agency.

Research Project

Write up your own application to be an astronaut. What qualities do you have that would make you a good one? In what science would you want to specialize? Look at different sciences to find your favorite.

Tools of the Trade

Scientists need gear to succeed. If they work in a laboratory, look for test tubes, computers, lasers, measuring instruments, microscopes, and more. Astronaut scientists use some of those things, but since they work in the gravity-free world of space, they also depend on very unique pieces of gear to do their jobs.

Spacesuit

When scientists are aboard the ISS, they wear soft, comfortable clothing. Sweatshirts, polo shirts, warmup pants, and socks work best. When they have to go outside to work on the space station, such as

WORDS TO UNDERSTAND

deforestation   the destruction of forest or woodland

extravehicular   something that happens outside a vehicle, in this case a space station

vacuum   the absence of air

when Dr. Marshburn saved the day by fixing the gas leak on that mission in 2013, they wear a spacesuit.

Astronauts love to use nicknames or acronyms for their gear. What you call a spacesuit, they call an EMU. That stands for **extravehicular** mobility unit, which means they wear it when they go outside the space station. The EMU is like a personal spacecraft. It weighs more than 300 pounds, but since zero gravity means zero weight, astronauts can "carry" the suits easily.

A large backpack provides oxygen to breathe. A device also scrubs out the carbon dioxide, the gas that humans breathe out. The backpack also has a cooling system. Space can be very cold, so the suit is heavy and protects from that. However, working in the direct sun can make it very hot. To prevent that, a cooling system sends liquid flowing through tubes in the suit.

The helmet has sunscreens to protect from harsh rays. The astronaut can also look at a computer readout that shows how the suit is working. It's always good to know how much air you have left when you're floating in space! The helmets also have communications gear that lets the space walker talk to fellow astronauts on and off the station, as well as with controllers on the ground. A bag of water with a straw lets astronauts get a drink if they need it.

What about going to the bathroom? The space suit helps with that, too. Astronauts wear special diapers or other devices so they can do what they need to do. Taking off the huge spacesuit just to go to the bathroom wouldn't make much sense!

Each piece of the suit connects with a tight seal. To survive in space, the astronaut must be completely covered. With the high-tech EMU, walking in space can be (almost!) a walk in the park.

By using the glove box, scientists working on the ISS remain safe while working with dangerous substances. Here an astronaut reaches into the rubber sleeves to work with an experiment in the box.

Glove Box

Back inside the station, an astronaut scientist has many work stations. He or she is probably in charge of several experiments. They are located in different places in the station, so the scientist floats from place to place to work on them.

Some experiments involve flame or gases. To work on such things, scientists use a "glove box." This large cube is built into the side of the station. From a small platform, the scientist puts his or her hands into thick gloves that extend into the cube through a wall. The scientist can then touch, move, and work with things inside the box, safe from danger.

The atmosphere inside the box can be changed for some experiments, for example, by adding nitrogen or creating a **vacuum**. Video recorders capture all the steps of the work so that later experts can learn from it.

Robotic Arm

For more than 30 years, scientists on board the ISS could thank Canada for giving them a hand . . . robotically! The Canadian Space Agency developed the versatile and amazing Canadarm. This long robotic arm extended from the space station. It could reach out

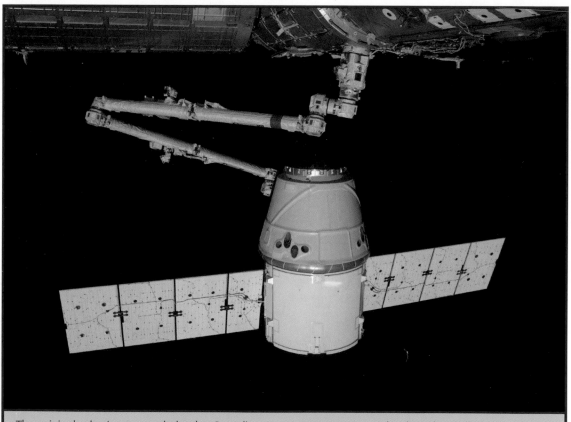

The original robotic arm made by the Canadian Space Agency was used to launch satellites like this one. Astronauts controlled the arm from inside the International Space Station.

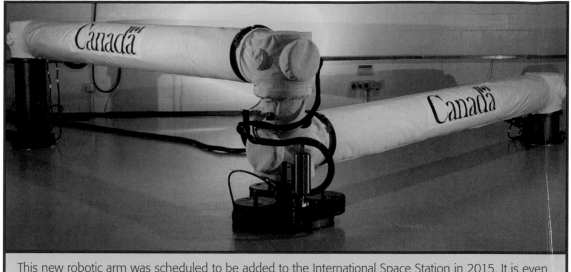
This new robotic arm was scheduled to be added to the International Space Station in 2015. It is even more versatile than the original.

and grab satellites that need repositioning. Astronauts could stand on the arm and be moved into positions around the station to work. Images taken from the arm's cameras let controllers on the ground observe the station in action.

Like many parts of the space program, Canadarm helped on Earth, too. The skills and techniques engineers learned making it helped them develop new robot tools for surgeons. Patients cared for by those surgeons can also give Canada a hand!

In 2013, the Canadarm was retired from service. A new robot arm created by the European Space Agency will take over. This crane-like robot will play a big part in the expansion of the station in years to come.

Looking Down

*M*any of the scientists on the space station are actually looking at Earth for their work. Photos and video taken from space help scientists who are studying weather, the oceans, the

Using a high-powered camera lens, this astronaut in the space station cupola has an amazing view of the Earth, spinning hundreds of miles below him.

atmosphere, and even earthquakes. The astronaut-scientists have an amazing view that adds greatly to their knowledge.

One of the best places to take the pictures and videos is from the "cupola." This cone-shaped spot on the bottom of the station has numerous windows on all sides. A scientist can sit in this space for hours and observe and learn as the Earth spins past at 1,000 miles (1,600 km) per hour. Special cameras inside the cupola take excellent nighttime images. Other cameras use infrared lenses. These cut out most of the light that lets us see things. What is left is usually invisible infrared light, but this special camera makes it visible. Studying infrared images can reveal unseen patterns on Earth. From these images and observations, scientists learn about everything from electrical usage to **deforestation**.

Where They Work

Without gravity, astronauts float as they work. They use handholds to help them glide around.

Scientists on Earth don't have to worry about their gear floating away. Or floating away themselves. Scientists working in space have those problems and more. Outside the Earth's atmosphere, the gravity that holds us and everything else down does not work. Astronauts call it something like living underwater. Scientists heading to space have to learn to live and work while unconnected to the Earth.

On the space station, there are many straps and bars astronauts can hook to. This helps them remain stable to work. That also means they can work on the floor, the walls, or the ceiling with no difficulty. There is no "up" in space. Even when "upside-down" to a camera viewer, astronauts do not feel like they are upside down.

Surviving in microgravity takes some practice. Astronauts, whether scientists or pilots, learn to move through the air by pulling themselves along. They learn the semi-crouched position that seems to help people be comfortable in zero Gs. Swallowing takes practice, since there is no gravity to help food down.

Brushing Teeth in Space!

Living in space calls for some interesting new ways to do things. Astronauts living on the space station still need to brush their teeth. However, there are no sinks—they have to use straws to get water. Toothpaste flows up to the brush. Then it's back to basics, brushing as on Earth. To rinse, most astronauts just take a sip of water, swish, and swallow. They can't spit it out. Water escaping into the cabin of the ship could damage sensitive equipment.

From brushing teeth to eating food in a bag, from sleeping stuck to a wall to using a special toilet, life for scientists in space is a series of challenges!

As for their scientific work, that is usually a bit easier. The experiments they perform were designed to work without gravity. In fact, part of many such experiments is finding out how zero gravity changes things.

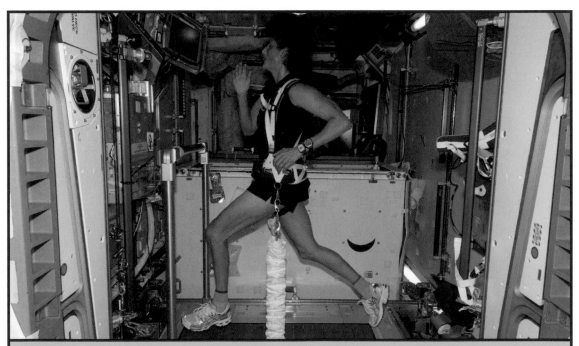

Just because you're in space, doesn't mean you don't have to exercise. Here an astronaut runs on a treadmill. Straps hold her down so that her feet can push against the treadmill.

Returning to Earth after months in zero gravity can be tricky, too. Canadian astronaut Chris Hadfield said he had to learn to talk again. "I hadn't realized that I had learned to talk with a weightless tongue," he said. Also, his body was sore, as it started using muscles it had not been using. "It feels like I played full-contact hockey, but it's getting better by the hour," he told reporters not long after landing in 2013.

Actually, to help those muscles, all astronauts—scientists included—have to exercise two hours a day. They use devices like bicycles, a treadmill, and even a weightlifting machine to make sure their muscles keep working.

 # Text-Dependent Questions

1. What problems did astronaut Chris Hadfield have on returning to Earth?

2. What do astronauts call their spacesuits?

3. What is the tool scientists use to handle dangerous experiments on the space station?

 # Research Project

Time to hit the pool! To see what life is like in zero gravity, take a swim. Pretend to brush your teeth underwater. Or try to put on a pair of sneakers (use old ones that will dry!). Or change your shirt. Swimming underwater is a good way to feel sort of like what astronauts feel.

Tales From the Field!

Moon Rocks!

*T*he Moon is a giant rock, so it made sense that a geologist should study it. Geology is the study of rocks and minerals, on Earth and other places. In 1965, Harrison Schmitt (on the Moon at left) was one of the first scientist-astronauts. Schmitt was working as a geologist in 1964 when he applied to be an astronaut. He had worked with another rocks expert from NASA and was inspired to try to get to the Moon.

He was selected and went through a year of training. Schmitt had to learn survival techniques, how rockets worked, and many other astronaut skills. He didn't learn to fly the rocket, however!

WORDS TO UNDERSTAND

biochemist a scientist who studies the chemistry of living things

carbon dioxide the type of gas that is in the air that we breathe out

pulsars a type of distant star that sends out radio waves

This closeup image of Moon rocks was taken during Apollo 17's mission. A hammer used by Schmitt to gather samples can be seen toward the bottom of the image.

Then he worked with other astronauts so that they could be "acting" geologists on the first Moon missions. By training his fellow space travelers to see some of what he could see in the rocks and dust of the Moon, he expanded the team's ability to bring science back to Earth.

In 1972, Schmitt was part of the last manned mission to our nearest neighbor. After landing on the Moon in Apollo 17, Schmitt explored the surface. He was the first to discover evidence of volcanoes on the Moon. He gathered rocks and took pictures of the various rock features. Having a real expert on hand added greatly to our knowledge of how the Moon was formed.

Torch in Space!

*L*eading up to the 2014 Winter Olympics, Russian cosmonaut Sergei Ryazansky took part in a special space walk. Ryazansky trained as a **biochemist**. His main job on the space station was to put in gear that would help monitor earthquakes on Earth. For this 2013 space walk, however, he carried something else: the Olympic torch. The Winter Games were to be held in Sochi, Russia. The Russian space group sent a torch up with its cosmonauts. On November 9, Ryazansky and Oleg Kotov carried the torch into space for the first time. It was not lit, since without oxygen, fire cannot burn in space.

The Olympic torch returned from its journey to space in 2013. It continued on a long journey that ended at the Opening Ceremonies of the 2014 Winter Olympics in Russia.

SkyLab

The International Space Station has been in use since 1981, but it was not the first space station. That honor goes to SkyLab, which first welcomed visitors in 1974. One of the first visitors to SkyLab was the first doctor in space, Joseph Kerwin.

SkyLab was created as a first step to learning how humans could live in space. The station was much smaller than the ISS, but had enough gear for numerous experiments.

For example, Dr. Kerwin took many measurements of his fellow astronauts, Pete Conrad and Joseph Wetiz. He could chart what changes their bodies underwent in space. The crew also worked with materials such as metal and ceramics, as well as lasers. Students on Earth also chipped in with experiments about plant growth, volcano studies, and rays from **pulsars**.

Two more missions to SkyLab carried other scientists into orbit. The structure did not last long, however. After removing all the key gear, NASA let SkyLab plunge to Earth in 1979. Most of it burned up on the way down, but some small pieces did smack into land.

Space Zoo

Doctors study how humans react to space travel, but what about other animals? Several space shuttle missions carried animals into space. Scientists watched the animals carefully. Tadpoles born in zero gravity, for instance, later hatched on Earth but did not survive. Born in zero-G, they did not know up or down, thus could not swim. Mice and monkeys flew on shuttle missions, too. Scientists found that the mice did just fine. "Within five minutes, mice are floating in

Skylab was the first permanent space station, in which scientists were able to do experiments that would eventually lead to the building of the larger International Space Station.

These tubes hold living fruit flies, which were among the many types of animals that have lived on board the ISS. Scientists work with the animals to learn how they adapt to life in space.

their living spaces, grooming themselves, and eating, just as they would on Earth," said NASA scientist Laura Lewis on NASA.com.

The monkeys did not have their appetite and did not enjoy weightlessness. Bees didn't mind at all. A colony of more than 3,000 bees continued to build their hive as if they were on Earth.

Some fish were carried into space to see if animals could reproduce. These fish did just fine, which might mean a way to create food sources on very, very long future flights.

Other scientists studied the effects of space on animals at the level of cells or studied microorganisms that were brought aboard.

A Space Green Thumb

*I*n the future, when astronauts want a salad with their dinner, they might be able to pick it themselves. Many missions have studied how plants grow in space. For example, plants move nutrients through their stems in part with gravity. Can they adapt to zero-G and still survive? Over the years, scientists have studied numerous plants in space. The latest is in a microwave-sized box called Veggie. Planted with lettuce seedlings, Veggie will live on the ISS. Special lights in the box provide the right energy.

"I was all smiles watching Commander Steve Swanson harvest his

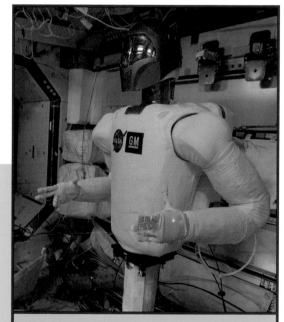

Robonaut was developed to help astronauts with dangerous or boring jobs!

Robonaut

Robotics is another science that is hard at work in space. It's a science that is in action on the space station right now. One crew member is working harder than others, 24 hours a day. It's Robonaut, the robot astronaut.

NASA developed Robonaut in hopes that robots can do some of the more dangerous or boring jobs needed in space. Robots can work around the clock and don't need to be fed or to use the bathroom! They can also work in dangerous environments, such as airless areas or even in areas with dangerous gases.

Robonaut on the ISS helps maintain some of the station's gear. It is programmed to check on various parts and report any problems. With hands like a human's, it can grab, carry, and hold gear. NASA is working on putting legs and feet on Robonaut in the future. Robot scientists, there's a place in space for you, too!

space lettuce," said NASA's Trent Smith after Veggie produced the first plants in 2014.

The gardening experiment will not only help by providing food. The plants will draw **carbon dioxide** from the cabin air—and the astronauts might enjoy practicing a little space gardening.

Fire in Space

Fire is a big part of space flight. After all, without powerful, flaming rockets, astronauts would not reach beyond our atmosphere. Once in space, fire is rare, since there is no oxygen, which fire needs to burn. Still, fire can happen inside the space station or space shuttle, since air in there lets the astronauts breathe. Fire safety is a very big part of training. Every astronaut, scientist or not, has to learn what to do and where to go in case of a fire on board. Just like in school, they practice with fire drills.

While fire is a danger, it is also a source of some important onboard experiments by astronaut/scientists. Scientists use the glove box (page 25) to burn small items and study the results. For instance, close images of flame in space show that the air around the flame moves differently in zero-G than on Earth. Knowing how fire burns in zero-G also teaches experts how to put out any possible fires.

"Astronauts are all very excited to do our [fire] experiments because space fires really do look quite alien," NASA engineer Dan Dietrich told *Smithsonian Magazine*. Why alien? Fire on Earth moves with gravity along with the oxygen in the air. Without gravity, the flame follows the oxygen in more random patterns. Where a match on Earth produces a teardrop-shaped flame, in space, the shape can be quite varied. Special cameras also show that the heat in space flame varies greatly, too.

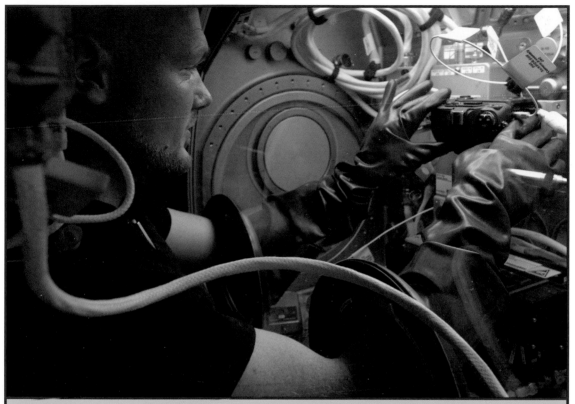

The only way to safely handle fire on board the ISS is by the use of the glove box. Here an astronaut with his arms in protective black gloves studies how flame behaves in zero gravity.

Subject: Scientist

*S*cientists in space have another way to experiment: on themselves. Astronauts are monitored in many ways so that experts back on Earth can track their health. They keep track of their heart rates, blood pressure, eating habits, and sleeping patterns. They are carefully measured before, during, and after their visits to space to better understand how being in space affects a person.

One thing that has been learned during the years humans have been going to space is the importance of exercise. When a person goes into space for a long time, their muscles and bones do not grow the

The scientists themselves are the subject of many of their experiments. How do their bodies react to life in space? How does exercise change "up there"? What they learn will shape future missions.

same way as on Earth. Also, because a person's muscles are not used for walking, standing, or moving (it's all that floating around they do!), those muscles can become weaker. To prevent this, the astronauts all have to work out every day.

They use a special exercise bicycle or a treadmill. To walk on the treadmill, they have to be strapped in. They can also use a machine that simulates weightlifting. It uses hydraulics to provide resistance in the same way weights work on Earth.

All this working out is one long experiment . . . but it also makes the astronauts feel pretty good, too.

The things that humans can learn from science in space are almost as wide and varied as space itself. The work of talented and brave scientists-turned-astronauts is changing our views of the world and making life better now and in the future. Anyone interested in just about any science can look to the stars for their possible future laboratory!

# Text-Dependent Questions

1. Why doesn't fire burn in space outside a space station?
2. How did mice react to living in zero gravity?
3. What was the name of the first space station?

Research Project

Students have contributed several experiments to NASA. Can you think of and research a new experiment that could be done in space? What do you hope to learn from this experiment?

Scientists in the News

Scientists-turned-astronauts have been in the news often over the years. Here are a few more stories of scientists who have used time in space—either by themselves or by sending experiments aloft—to make new discoveries.

Searching for Sprites: Japanese researcher Dr. Mitsuteru Sato created an experiment to search for sprites and elves. Not the kind from fairy tales, though—those are names given to atmospheric displays inside storms. Sato built a machine to detect and examine these displays, and it was successfully used on the ISS in 2013.

Surviving Space: The ISS and other spacecraft are made of dozens of types of materials: metals, plastics, fabrics, and more. Knowing how well those sort of things will survive and function in space is a key part of astronaut safety. In 2014, NASA's Kim de Groh won an award for the studies her team did on a wide variety of materials.

Taking a Dive: NASA astronaut/scientist Jeannette Epps has not gone to space yet, but she has gotten a lot of practice . . . underwater. Epps joined a 2014 mission called NEEMO that was designed to study how people could live in extreme conditions. Instead of going to space, this former physics student lived 62 feet (18.9 m) beneath the Atlantic Ocean for nine days. She and three other astronauts (or were they aquanauts?) did a number of dives meant to simulate space walks. They also practiced communicating via radio and learned how their bodies adjusted to living in small spaces.

The SpaceX Dragon capsule will someday be used to shuttle a pair of astronauts to and from the ISS.

Astronauts at Work: In 2014, NASA announced that it was signing two companies to create spacecraft that would take future astronauts to the ISS. Boeing has long been a part of the NASA team; it employs thousands of scientists, and these new craft will open up new opportunities. The other company is new: SpaceX. It was created by Elon Musk, the man who started the Tesla electric car company. The SpaceX "Dragon" craft can carry two people and a host of gear to the ISS. Flights for both companies are supposed to start in 2017. The work of scientists in space will continue far into the future!

Find Out More

Books

Gibson, Karen Bush. *Women in Space: 23 Stories of First Flights, Scientific Missions, and Gravity-Breaking Adventures.* Chicago: Chicago Review Press, 2013.

Halls, Kelly Milner. *Astronaut: 21st Century Skills Library.* North Mankato, Minn.: Cherry Lake Publishing, 2013.

Mara, Wil. *Space Exploration: Science, Technology, Engineering.* Danbury, Conn.: Children's Press, 2014.

Platt, Richard. *Galactic Mission: DK Adventures.* New York: DK Publishing, 2014. A novel based in fact about a long-distance space mission.

Web Sites

NASA NASA.com
This massive Web site takes you everywhere astronauts have gone. Learn about space flight, science experiments, and astronauts.

Smithsonian airandspace.si.edu
The Smithsonian's Air and Space Museum site is packed with historical photos and articles about space flight.

European Space Agency esa.int
Astronaut/scientists from a dozen European countries have been to the ISS. Read more about them here.

Series Glossary of Key Terms

airlock a room on a space station from which astronauts can move from inside to outside the station and back

anatomy a branch of knowledge that deals with the structure of organisms

bionic to be assisted by mechanical movements

carbon dioxide a gas that is in the air that we breathe out

classified kept secret from all but a few people in a government or an organization

deforestation the destruction of forest or woodland

diagnose to recognize by signs and symptoms

discipline in science, this means a particular field of study

elite the part or group having the highest quality or importance

genes information stored in cells that determine a person's physical characteristics

geostationary remaining in the same place above the Earth during an orbit

innovative groundbreaking, original

inquisitiveness an ability to be curious, to continue asking questions to learn more

internships jobs often done for free by people in the early stages of study for a career

marine having to do with the ocean

meteorologist a scientist who forecasts weather and weather patterns

physicist a scientist who studies physics, which examines how matter and energy move and relate

primate a type of four-limbed mammal with a developed brain; includes humans, apes, and monkeys

traits a particular quality or personality belonging to a person

Index

Photo Credits

All images are courtesy of NASA with the following notes:

12: NASA/Paolov Nespoli

19: NASA/Gagarin Cosmonaut Training Center

32: NASA/Eugene Cernan

41: NASA/ESA

45: NASA/Dimitri Gerondidakis

Scientists in Action logo by Comicraft.

About the Author

K.C. Kelley has written dozens of nonfiction books for young readers on topics as wide as space: animals, nature, robots, baseball, history, careers, and, of course, astronauts.